# OVERTHINKING TAKEOVER

7 Powerful Ways to a Joyful and Vibrant Self

JAPJOT KANG

Chennai • Bangalore

CLEVER FOX PUBLISHING
Chennai, India

Published by CLEVER FOX PUBLISHING 2024
Copyright © Japjot Kang 2024

All Rights Reserved.
ISBN: 978-93-67079-62-1

This book has been published with all reasonable efforts taken to make the material error-free after the consent of the author. No part of this book shall be used, reproduced in any manner whatsoever without written permission from the author, except in the case of brief quotations embodied in critical articles and reviews.

The Author of this book is solely responsible and liable for its content including but not limited to the views, representations, descriptions, statements, information, opinions and references ["Content"]. The Content of this book shall not constitute or be construed or deemed to reflect the opinion or expression of the Publisher or Editor. Neither the Publisher nor Editor endorse or approve the Content of this book or guarantee the reliability, accuracy or completeness of the Content published herein and do not make any representations or warranties of any kind, express or implied, including but not limited to the implied warranties of merchantability, fitness for a particular purpose. The Publisher and Editor shall not be liable whatsoever for any errors, omissions, whether such errors or omissions result from negligence, accident, or any other cause or claims for loss or damages of any kind, including without limitation, indirect or consequential loss or damage arising out of use, inability to use, or about the reliability, accuracy or sufficiency of the information contained in this book.

# Contents

*Acknowledgements ................................................. iv*
*Introduction ............................................................ v*

Chapter 1: Which Way Is The Bus Going? ................. 1
Chapter 2: Thinking And Remembering .................... 3
Chapter 3: the Existing and the Living Zone.............. 7
Chapter 4: Attitude Is The Key to Success ................ 10
Chapter 5: Inventory ............................................... 16
Chapter 6: What Will People Say? .......................... 27
Chapter 7: Sufferings And Overthinking .................. 29
Chapter 8: The Master Problem-Solving Formula .... 31

*Epilogue .................................................................37*
*About the Author ...................................................40*
*Books in this Series ................................................41*
*Books By The Author .............................................44*

# Acknowledgements

*"I want to thank my parents and brother for supporting my ideas and vision of creating a better world."*

# Introduction

Mobile phones are considered one of the best human inventions ever. They are among the most sold pieces of consumer technology. I am sharing this information here because of what I will highlight next: 'Mobile Applications.' What are mobile applications? They are computer programs designed to run on mobile phones. Since they are computer programs, they need to be updated regularly to comply with all the advancements in our mobile phones. Otherwise, the applications will slow down, hang, or not work. We receive constant notifications to update them.

But what about our minds? We don't update them regularly. Otherwise, we keep running the same thinking patterns and continue living our lives with the same limitations, as there isn't a notification for the same. Now, isn't there something we can do to update our minds, regularly update their thinking patterns, banish our limitations, manage our emotions well, feel great, make the best use of our time, and be well-prepared to face the world and different situations in our lives in a refurbished way?

That's where this book comes in. It's the notification to update our minds. This book will empower us with simple tools and skills to diffuse old thinking patterns, overcome overthinking, and update to new patterns of joy, peace, and vibrancy, which will serve our best interests and prepare us well to face different situations in our day-to-day lives. So, we can finally experience a new, beautifully designed interface like the ones we experience with mobile apps that allow us to live the best of our lives. Just imagine how great that would be and how amazing that would feel.

No one ever told us something like this is possible, but I promise it is. Based on its effectiveness, every exercise and skill shared in the book is applied to me and others first and then supplied to you. The only prerequisite required to get a ton from this book is to approach it as a child who loves playing games as we did when we were a child; maybe we still do as I do. Let's trust ourselves; our inner child wants the best for us and knows we deserve it. So, let's be curious about what we'll learn from the book. Curiosity alone is the primary factor that makes learning more accessible for kids and not so simple for adults, as they are fascinated by the new information coming their way. So, let's access the "inner curious" within as we progress with the book.

*Introduction*

**"You must be curious about it to be good at it."**

**ANONYM0US**

Once we access this 'curiosity', we will open ourselves to a sky full of learning opportunities. Before we delve deep into the book chapters, I have a fun question for you.

**Q. When was the last time you laughed out loud?**

It could be a joke, a funny experience shared by someone, or something else that made you laugh hard. Try to feel what you felt at that time now and spend a couple of seconds with the feelings until you start to chuckle again.

Let's start the book with the lovely combination of two C's - curiosity and a chuckle, and make the learning that comes our way simple, exciting, and fun.

# CHAPTER 1

# WHICH WAY IS THE BUS GOING?

Let's talk about a scenario where James takes a specific bus route to commute from his house to his workplace; let's refer to it as route number 22, a straight 35-minute route with three stops. He had been successfully using this route for over five years until one day when he was late from work and boarded a different bus that was leaving and heading in the same direction as the route number 22 bus. Unknowingly, he observed the bus turning left and right, unable to understand what was happening until he realised he was on the wrong bus. He alighted at the first stop after 15 minutes, as that's what we all would do if we knew we were not heading towards our intended destination.

The purpose of sharing this small scenario was to draw our attention to the fact that the same applies to our minds when constantly overthinking various aspects of life. We should disembark from the bus but remain aboard, unaware of its destination. Unintentionally, it veers off course and leads us to an unfamiliar place we never intended to visit. Now that our minds dictate our paths, how can we ensure we steer them towards the correct destinations? The simple solution is to learn how to influence our minds and ensure we head in the right direction.

The chapters and the book's quick exercises will help us change the images and movies we play when we overthink. It's as simple as switching channels using a remote on a TV screen. It'll enable us to see images of what we want and feel good about it, regaining all the time we would lose on the imaginary sufferings in our heads and feeling unpleasant about them.

We'll be able to do so much more with all the time we will regain as most of the time in our lives. "It takes less time to do something than we invest in overthinking about it," and we'll be able to influence our day-to-day lives. A day at a time is all we need to start changing our lives, not a week, a month, or an entire year.

## CHAPTER 2

# THINKING AND REMEMBERING

Before diving deep into the chapter, let's learn about three terms first.

**Thinking** - Thinking is using one's mind to produce thoughts.

**Remembering** - Remembering is the ability to recall information from our memory.

**Overthinking** is when our thoughts and worries circle in an endless loop.

Our thinking is comprised of three parts –

## Past | Present | Future

If we prioritise what we should spend the most of our time on over others, the answer will be the present, without a doubt. We will have the answer to why by the end of this chapter.

> **"Remember to live in the present; the past is history, and the future can wait."**
>
> ANONYMOUS

If we carefully look at the word Present, it's a combination of two words **pre-sent**. It means it is sent to us based on our dominant past thinking patterns, emotions, feelings, actions. That's fine, as we will soon learn the quick tools to take charge of our old patterns of mind, leverage the present moment, and make the most out of our future. If we learn to do some quick things and appreciate the present as a gift, it's supposed to be as both the words present and gift are synonymous; imagine for a couple of seconds how fantastic our future would be.

Doing so will enable us to enjoy and embrace the most essential asset or commodity of our lives: **time.** Another thing that strengthens our belief in the importance of the present moment is sharing what I call the car mirrors metaphor. Have you ever wondered why a car's rearview mirror is way too small compared to the gigantic windshield and what it has to do with our lives? One can't drive without crashing if the focus is solely on the rearview mirror. That's akin to life; we can't function well if all we do is look back and dwell on our past.

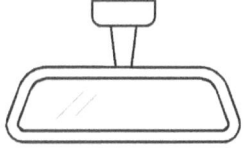 

Sure, it would be great if we looked at all the pleasant stuff from the past, making us feel good about it often, but that is not the case. As humans, we are programmed to lose connections quite quickly to our pleasant memories and firmly hold on to the unpleasant ones, and we can't seem to let go of them, but it will change soon. So, what we learn from the car mirrors metaphor is to focus on the windshield most of the time and appreciate what is being presented in our lives.

**Q. How easy or difficult is it to appreciate the present moment?**

The answer is simple: take a deep breath and appreciate a few things around you, to the left, right, above, and below. It could be a window on the left offering a view of the outside world, a closet on the right holding your daily essentials, a ceiling fan above providing you with air, or some comfortable footwear below. It might also be the clothes you're wearing or something else - there's plenty to choose from. Take a moment to acknowledge three things around you before moving on to the next question in this chapter.

**Q.** What do you spend most of your time thinking about?

# CHAPTER 3

# THE EXISTING AND THE LIVING ZONE

We live our day-to-day lives primarily operating in two zones: the existing zone and the living zone. We can easily distinguish between the two based on one's words, feelings, and actions at any given time.

An individual who primarily belongs to the existing zone, also known as the getting-by zone, is someone who frequently complains about different things in life, finds reasons not to smile, overthinks all the imaginary what-if scenarios, looks for things that are missing and not good in their life, usually problem-oriented, perceives the future as uncertain, lacks energy, isn't kind to themselves, and reflects the same on others. Existing means surviving without truly experiencing the emotions and feelings within it. One may live in the past or the future but only exist in the present.

On the other hand, living means the existence of a being up to the fullest. This implies that you are not just breathing to exist; each breath imparts life's sense and fragrance. An individual who primarily resides in the living zone, also known as the 'making the best of it' zone, appreciates things in life, actively seeks reasons to smile, and anticipates opportunities in the future. They usually believe that things will work out in their favour, focus on solutions, maintain a high energy level, and show kindness to themselves and others. One truly embarks on living when grateful for current possessions and thankful for what lies ahead. What truly matters in leading a 'living life' is letting go of past experiences and the expectations they have set for the future.

It's crucial not to be swayed by the illusions we create about life. We can avoid conforming to the pace of others who might be too busy to live genuinely. It's about finding our rhythm and living on our terms. Suppose one is primarily in the existing zone or somehow swinging between the two. In that case, they can rest assured that they can make quick yet transformative shifts in their life by following some simple and fun exercises in Chapter Five.

*The Existing and The Living Zone*

"Remember, there is no perfect time for anything. There is only now."

JACK CANFIELD

Q. Which zone would you primarily like to live your life from?

## CHAPTER 4

# ATTITUDE IS THE KEY TO SUCCESS

"Attitude is a little thing that makes a big difference."

**WINSTON CHURCHILL**

*E*veryone experiences not-so-good stuff, but why does one's reaction to an external event seem relatively neutral? In contrast, why does another individual's response seem like something gigantic happened to them?

It is because of the attitude they possess at the very moment. Let's read the story of two brothers to understand more about it. Two brothers lived in a small town. One day, suddenly, their house caught fire due to some electrical failure. Not knowing what the right thing could be to do due to the panicky situation, both brothers ran out and saved their lives. More than half of their house got burned down, but both didn't face any physical injuries, and that's a good thing. Now, both had different attitudes towards what happened to them.

One complained about the situation and looked out for all the material things he lost in the fire, while the other appreciated that they were alive and nothing had happened to them. That's the key takeaway from this situation: tangible things can return, but what about life? You either have it or you don't. Let's talk about another scenario involving two employees. They worked on a presentation they had to deliver to their team's manager.

After the presentation, the team manager shared her feedback. She knew they could do a much better job if they tried and were unsatisfied with their presentation. One employee shared his takeaway with his colleagues: She had the same old stuff to say about my work regardless of how or if I didn't work. He hoped the manager would get replaced soon and whatnot.

On the contrary, the other employee seemed unaffected, as if he hadn't faced the same situation as the first employee. When his colleagues asked why he appeared fine while his partner for the presentation was complaining and blaming the manager for this situation, he replied that he appreciated the feedback they got from her, as that allowed him to learn and grow. He now knows what to avoid and ensure for the next presentation. According to his positive attitude, "There's no failure, only feedback."

In the above two scenarios, we have learnt how individuals' attitudes vary based on where they're focusing. Bad things happen to everyone; no one's immune to it and can't control it, but we can control and influence how we react. Always remember-

**"A bad day doesn't equal a bad life."**

**ANONYMOUS**

The quick exercises in the next chapter will help us establish a positive attitude by letting go of all those unpleasant experiences and memories we've held on to for a long time. We think about them now and then and wonder if they hadn't happened, life would have been better. We'll be working on replacing those only ifs with positive and pleasant things from our lives.

But before moving on to the next chapter, let's review some pointers for instantly shifting our attitude and forming a more positive one.

# 1. Change our words

Our attitude can be influenced by how we talk about events. For example, we'll keep thinking negatively when we speak negatively about something. Be that as it may, we'll change our views if you discuss it positively. Words like "I can't do that" or "That's complex' encourage us to maintain that viewpoint. You will probably believe what you say is impossible. "I can do this if I take it step by step" or "That's doable" are examples of positive words. Don't let our words work against us; let them work for us instead. First, we change our label about something; it changes our thoughts and feelings about it, and then it reflects in our actions and determines the quality of the results we get out of life.

So this is how this simple equation works-

**Label -> Thoughts -> Feelings > Actions -> Results**

It's entirely up to us how we'd like to label different things in our lives. If we don't do well in any area, please check the labels and see how we can change them and make positive shifts.

## 2. Be proactive rather than reactive.

We have a second option in every situation. We can whine or take care of our concerns. While complaining makes us unhappy, acting always improves the situation. It instils in us a feeling of usefulness and achievement.

For instance, Marc is driving to work, having his morning coffee, and trying to answer a phone call when he accidentally spills it over the car floor. His instant reaction is, "I know it's just not my day, and it is just the beginning of all I will go through today." Instead, he could be proactive and state, 'It's a message for me not to try doing multiple things simultaneously. I know it'll be a good day regardless of this event.'

## 3. Possess an attitude of gratitude

It teaches us to appreciate the good things in our lives; gratitude is essential to having a positive attitude. Practising gratitude teaches us to focus on the positive rather than the negative. It sounds easier said than done, but when was the last time we took some time to be grateful towards our loved ones and appreciate their presence in our lives, the vehicle that drives us to work, the meals we eat, or someone who has prepared them for us? Such little things that we have lost connection with over time and started taking for granted. We could identify three things we appreciate daily, take a minute or two, and say thank you internally. This practice will immensely help us maintain a positive attitude.

## 4. Focusing on the small pleasures in our lives

Most people constantly focus on their big goals and anticipate their next vacation or holiday. Even though looking ahead is not necessarily bad, it can sometimes make us forget the good things in our everyday lives. If we only think about the future, we would be unable to appreciate these small pleasures, like a cup of our favourite coffee or a conversation with an old friend, playing a sport we enjoy, and many more. Hence, we try to be present in the moment and enjoy these small pleasures of our lives. Following these simple tips will help us build a positive attitude almost instantly, which will be reflected in our day-to-day conversations and actions.

> **"You can stop anything but a person with a good attitude."**
>
> **RICHARD BANDLER**

**Q. What attitude would you focus primarily on in your daily life?**

## CHAPTER 5

# INVENTORY

> "The secret of change is to focus all your energy, not on fighting the old, but on building the new."
>
> **SOCRATES**

*W*elcome to my favourite chapter of the book. It's not the end of the book; I've saved the best for the last chapter. It's my favourite because it helps one achieve results in life and empowers one to let go of all the only ifs (only if it wouldn't have happened, then I would have) and the what-ifs (what if this or that happens) from their lives.

Inventory is a complete list of items, such as goods in stock. But the type of inventory I'm referring to here is mental inventory. Mental inventory stands for the cognitive tools we already have at our disposal. Our mind has registered and stored all the pleasant and unpleasant memories and everything we have experienced so far in life. We have learned to be very good at imagining all the what-ifs in the future and overthinking them all day, affecting our present moment. Our minds are very good at filtering out and building strong connections to the unpleasant ones and losing connections to the pleasant ones. That's why we hold on to arguments and confrontations for long and quickly lose connections to appreciation and compliments.

The three quick (under four minutes) yet powerful exercises will enable us to unlearn this automated repetitive pattern and learn about all the great stuff instead. All we'd need is a memory or a past event to free ourselves from. More of it will make sense when we go through the short description for each exercise, determining which one is best for which scenario.

All this chapter is about is replacing not-so-pleasant things with pleasant ones and freeing us from the past turmoil to build a bright and exciting future for us as we'll essentially learn to see our present as an "opportunity" it is.

Before starting the exercises, let's establish a couple of prerequisites. Please ensure you complete each exercise at least twice; they are just under four minutes long. Expect improvement with each repetition. Remember to strive for progress, not perfection, as perfection is unattainable. Remember that no one becomes proficient at something on their first try. If someone claims otherwise, they're likely not truthful. A brief description and the steps involved will accompany each exercise.

# 1. Image Minimizer

> **"The easier you can make it inside your head, the easier it will make things outside your head."**
>
> **RICHARD BANDLER**

Going through this quote made me think, hmm…. does it work like this? I was amazed at how true it was, and I came up with the image minimiser exercise. It worked wonders for me and others I got to try it on. Now I'm sharing it with all of you.

Our mind communicates and understands the language of images. Carefully read the following sentence twice: **"A cat sat on the mat.**" Essentially, our mind creates images of the same. Your cat and mat might differ from someone else's, but this is how our mind works. Whenever we or someone else is communicating about something complicated, challenging, complex, or similar, our mind unknowingly creates huge images of the same. When we discuss easy and doable things, we unconsciously create small-sized mental images. So, if we can intentionally train our minds to shrink significant images, our perception shifts. The things we perceive as challenging will now seem achievable.

The best scenarios to work with for this exercise could be a complex project at work, playing a challenging sport, or something you consider difficult. It will help you make it more straightforward and doable, so you'll be able to perform well on it. Yes, it is that easy. Follow all the steps sequentially before closing your eyes to reap the benefits. Repeat the word 'focus' five times and take two slow, deep breaths to centre your attention on the present moment.

**Let's get started with the eyes-closed exercise –**

1. You can bring up an image of something you consider challenging or complex and notice its size; it could be on the left or right side, near or far. Try to get a sense of where that huge image is.
2. Now, bring an image of something you consider easy to do or something you do daily, like preparing coffee in the morning or tying your shoelaces, and notice where its image is located and its small size.
3. Now, take the large image and make it similar to the small image and observe how your perception and feelings towards that object change. Once you have completed the step, you are done.

Please try to repeat this exercise at least twice and get used to it. We can use it for multiple purposes in our lives.

Even the slightest change initially is beneficial, guiding us in a positive direction. "Things aren't necessarily hard or easy; our perception of them makes them seem so." For example, I never excelled or performed adequately when dealing with Pythagoras' theorem. However, this does not indicate the same for everyone in the class; perhaps I underestimated its significance. I believe this exercise could have been beneficial in the past, and I am relieved to have this knowledge now as it can quickly shift one's perspective in just a few minutes.

The logic behind the exercise is quite simple: whenever someone tells you something is challenging, notice the image you're forming. You know how to deal with the new ones and all the past ones you already have in your mind. Just start by making these images smaller and smaller, as this works on shifting our perception and changing how we think. If we can shift our thinking about it, then-.

**Thinking -> Feelings -> Actions -> Results**

Results are the name of the game, as results are the very reason we do what we do every day in different areas of our lives.

## 2. Whiteout and Blissful Images Exercise

The second exercise has two parts: the whiteout and the blissful images. Let's go through the part one first. The best scenario where this exercise comes in handy is when you're continuously running images of what may go wrong or has gone wrong in the past in your head. As you now know, images are the language of your mind, so whenever you catch yourself stuck in a pattern of overthinking, try to get hold of the images you are making in your head.

Use the whiteout image method to shift your focus towards something positive and bright immediately. As where your focus goes, it expands and multiplies into more unpleasant stuff if you don't do anything about it. You're just about to do the very thing about it now. Follow all the steps sequentially before closing your eyes to reap the benefits. Repeat the word 'focus' five times and take two slow, deep breaths to centre your attention on the present moment.

**Let's get started with the eyes-closed exercise –**

1. You can bring up an image of something bothering you and think about it. It could be something current, from the past, or some future event. Just notice where it's located in your mind. It could be on the left or

right, bottom or top. Frame the image inside your mind.
2. Now, as soon as you can spot the image, imagine yourself lifting a bucket full of white paint and splashing it on the image in your mind and seeing your image as a complete whiteout. Now, notice how your feelings are starting to shift. You can even repeat the splashing of the white paint step twice or thrice until you completely white out the image.
3. Now, notice the white screen in your mind and how your thinking and feelings have shifted. You can open your eyes after a few seconds.

Let's move on to part two of the exercise. Our minds are now filled with a blank screen, so how can we utilise this effectively? By replacing it with a joyful image. We can search our memory for a cheerful moment from the past; it might be something remarkable you wish to experience again, such as a birthday party, a kind word, a significant achievement like your graduation, or a memory that brightens your face with a smile. Although it is always within us, it often stays concealed in our mental archives. Reflect on that delightful memory. Once you have it, let's proceed to the next phase of the exercise.

1. Bring up an image of something blissful and bright from your past and place it where the whiteout screen was. Make it seem natural and as colourful as possible.

2. Next, you can see the image of this memory becoming bigger and bigger, like a movie theatre screen, and you can even step inside it to see what you saw back then, hear what you heard and feel how good you feel as if it's happening right now.
3. Notice how your thoughts and feelings shift due to a change in focus and feel all the pleasantness of the moment. After spending a minute or two there, you can open your eyes.

The idea behind the exercise is simple: whenever we see something in our minds that doesn't make us feel pleasant, we splash the white paint bucket on it and then have something extraordinary to play with. We have a stock full of such events from our lives. Wouldn't it be great if we intentionally learn to create such moments of bliss with different pleasant memories from our stock and replace them with the things we overthink in our lives and feel not so good? With this exercise, I'm sure it'd be.

**"Where focus goes, energy flows."**

**TONY ROBBINS**

This quote is valid for all of us, and I would even like to add two more words at the end: "Result shows."

Hence, "where focus goes, energy flows, and the result shows.'

## 3. Anxiety buster exercise

Welcome to the anxiety buster exercise. This exercise is best suited for situations where you feel anxious about things not working well or going wrong, thinking, 'I won't be able to do it.' It could be a presentation at work, an exam you fear, a difficult conversation at home, or something that makes you anxious and nervous.

Your mind has learned what anxiety means to you and how your body reacts to it. It is now programmed to see things in a way that does not work out for you. It knows how to manifest and show up in your body when we think of such an event. But you'll learn how to program your mind to focus on something pleasant and prepare well for it instead. The preparation starts in the mind first.

I want to share the "war metaphor" before the exercise begins. Why go to war when one believes winning isn't possible and have already accepted defeat? It's like when, as kids, we would play a game or a sport with someone familiar with it. How good did we feel then, knowing that our chances to win were next to none?

So, let's practice this exercise regularly to shift our focus towards the desirable. It will cause a shift in our feelings and lead to different actions; we will achieve a different result, and that's what we all need.

*Inventory*

# "By preparing to fail, you're preparing to fail."

## BENJAMIN FRANKLIN

Let's learn to prepare well now. In this exercise, "successful completion" refers to achieving better-than-expected outcomes from a particular event. Let's practice this concept with the following exercise. Pleasse refer to the image below.

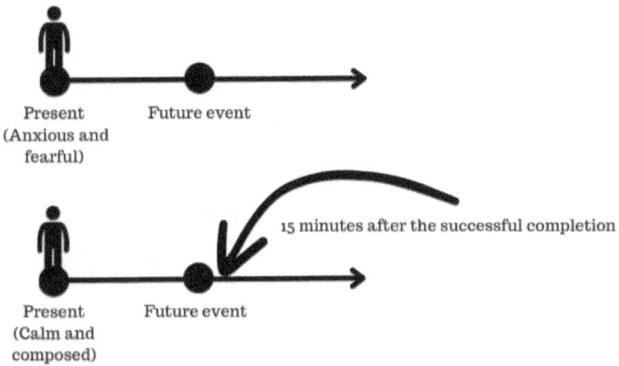

1. Imagine an image of a future event or something recurring that makes you feel anxious or nervous.
2. Secondly, notice the anxious feelings starting to build in your body as you think about this event for 30 seconds.
3. Finally, shift your focus to 15 minutes after the successful completion of the event. See what you'll see and hear what you'll hear. Notice the feelings inside

your body, knowing it went way better than expected. Stay with the new set of feelings for a couple of minutes.

Please repeat this exercise several times to get good at it.

Now, the question is how well you can prepare for an event if you shift your focus toward a favourable outcome. You have already programmed your mind to see it going wrong multiple times, and that's why it manifests in your reality. What if you program it to focus on the contrary instead, and how will this exercise shift your actions?

Now, we understand the significance of the mental images we create and their subsequent outcomes. Through the exercises, we have learned to modify them when they are not beneficial, saving time and energy. We can resize them, add a touch of white paint, or swap them with new, pleasant, positive, and vibrant ones.

**Q. What pleasant memory did you use in the second exercise? Connect with it once again and feel how good it made you feel.**

# CHAPTER 6

# WHAT WILL PEOPLE SAY?

"What will people say?" This sentence has killed more dreams than anything else in the world. Try not to squander a snapshot of our valuable lives, stressing over what others will think about us. Nothing decent can happen to it. We will waste far more energy imagining what other people think of us than they will ever put into it. Most people are too caught up in their lives to pay much attention to what others are doing. While we are stressing over their thought process, they agonise over others' thought processes. Simply stressing our lives away...

Rather than worrying about what others think, let's focus on what we believe about ourselves. No matter how wise, intelligent, or well-intentioned we think others are, our opinion of ourselves is more important than their opinion of us. Realise that other people's opinions about us are solely theirs and have little to do with us. We are genuinely unknowable to anyone, and we must live our lives. So overthinking and wasting time on it isn't worth it.

Another question I would like us to consider right now is how long people will talk about us. Will they talk about us for one year, five years, or ten years? Will they talk about us first thing in the morning or last thing before bed? I wonder if they only spoke about us rather than something essential or themselves. What will people around them think of them? Would people be interested in communicating with them as they have nothing else to discuss?

So, if we sense they can't talk about us for the rest of their lives, let's drop the idea of what they will think or say about us now. Let's be kind to ourselves and escape this imaginary monster off our backs. Always remember-

> **"People will say something regardless of whether we do something or not."**
>
> **"Care about other people's thoughts, and you will always be their prisoner."**
>
> **LAO TZU**

**Q. Would you still care about and be bothered by what others say or think about you?**

# CHAPTER 7

# SUFFERINGS AND OVERTHINKING

"Pain is inevitable. Suffering is optional."

HARUKI MURAKAMI

This saying applies to all of us. Since most events occur beyond our control, pain is inevitable and universal; however, our perspectives and reactions to challenges determine how much and for how long we will suffer. For example, we recall the story of two brothers from chapter four, where one brother accepted reality and appreciated the beauty around him, while the other focused on what was lost and absent from his life.

In times like these, one plans to blame and complain, and the other looks for things to appreciate and makes the most out of them. The difference between the two is the time (our most valuable asset) we lose or make the best use of. The fact is that we can get back resources like money, but what about time? It won't.

It seems significant to share a metaphor that I call the birthday present metaphor.

Not appreciating the present moment is like receiving a present on our birthday but insisting on opening it on our next birthday. We wouldn't do that with our birthday present because we'd be curious about what's in it. Let's consider our present moment and live it as a gift to ensure we are living a beautiful present that leads to an even more beautiful future.

Let's play a game for two minutes in which we appreciate at least five things around us now. It could be anything, from a glass of clean drinking water to your eyes or ears, with which you can go through this book now.

It's up to our focus to guide us; it'll multiply whether we blame, complain, or appreciate it. We will look for or manifest more events, things, and people to blame or complain about and feel terrible or appreciate and feel good. The choice is up to us to make. Which one would we go with? I can hear a loud one coming my way, and we know by now which one it would be.

# CHAPTER 8

# THE MASTER PROBLEM-SOLVING FORMULA

"The key is not the will to win… everybody has that. It is the will to prepare to win that is important."

**BOBBY KNIGHT**

Humans face challenges in their daily lives, and many tend to overthink them. However, some individuals quickly navigate these challenges and find solutions instead of complaining about their complexity. They may not be the smartest or most intelligent, but they possess the skill often called "thinking outside the box."

**"Think outside the box", but how?**

My two-word answer to possess it is - **"AS IF."**

The individuals who figure out how often they come up with solutions to a problem have taken reasonable control over these four primary things, mostly unknowingly. These are their -

- Internal dialogue
- Facial expressions
- Breathing patterns
- Spine and Shoulders

For instance, a challenging project arises at work that many can't figure out how to approach. On the other hand, individuals who generate potential solutions never perceive it as a challenge. They refer to it as a situation; their facial expressions remain unchanged, and they maintain good posture with upright spine and shoulders, resulting in a relaxed breathing pattern.

Another way to look at it is that all the best public speakers we've experienced, either in person or online have this in common. They all possess a great posture with an upright spine and shoulders, relaxed breathing, and excellent facial expressions caused by an empowering internal dialogue.

An excellent example of this is when one is feeling angry or confident. The difference between the two would be one's internal dialogue: one would be disempowering, and the other empowering. One would display unpleasant facial expressions, while the other would show pleasant ones.

One would exhibit a shallow breathing pattern, while the other would exhibit a deep one. Lastly, the spine and shoulders of one would be dropped, while those of the other would be upright.

**So, how can we learn to possess this zone on demand?**

The answer to this would be a simple one: try to make changes to these four things starting from our internal dialogue by using words like indeed, I will, and I can, as this will automatically make positive changes to our facial expressions, resulting in a relaxed breathing pattern and we'll have our spine and shoulders upright.

Let's say we must prepare for a presentation at work next week, and all we've been telling ourselves in our heads is that I'm not confident. How can one be optimistic while presenting?

Access the AS IF zone by closing your eyes and repeating 'As If I'm confident' around 10-15 times to yourself in your mind or even out loud. Start intentionally changing your facial expressions, breathing pattern, spine, and shoulders. You can repeat it more times until you have changed your thinking pattern. You'll soon notice a more empowered way of thinking about something by changing its label. We can practice it as often as we'd like with different useful labels.

**Label -> Thinking -> Feelings ->Actions -> Results**

With regular practice of the "AS IF" principle in our lives, we can become master problem solvers. It will make us solution-oriented and give us something at our command every time we use it. Regular practice of AS IF will make it automatic for us, becoming a part of our identity. Failure to comply will keep us stuck in old labels, leading to old thoughts, feelings, and actions with similar outcomes.

So whenever we find ourselves in situations where we'd like to come up with potential solutions, we can use the AS IF principle by making changes to the four vital elements of AS IF to think outside the box and open up our potential, which was limited before because of our label on it.

Let me share the "puzzle metaphor" that complements the AS IF principle. Two kids receive the same puzzles to solve. One kid labels it the most challenging task, while the other embodies the AS IF principle and eagerly anticipates tackling the puzzle. The second child will likely solve the puzzle first as he has already positioned himself as a winner, a mindset reflected in his results.

So, the AS IF principle will shift our focus from the problem to the solution and prompt us to think backwards about achieving the results as if we already know the answer. How would our thinking change? It unlocks our cognitive abilities and introduces a fresh perspective, often constrained by the limitations we have imposed through various labels in different situations.

This principle sounds too good to be accurate, but it is the shortest and surest way to unlock the powers of our actual mental faculties. Right from childhood, we're programmed so that we can or can't do something. We are always left limited because we can't imagine all that we can. We have never imagined what would happen if we could. I have a third question for us today: "AS IF you can". Notice the immediate sense of empowerment that comes with this phrase.

So, how can one make the most out of the AS IF? By making changes to four key elements –

- Internal dialogue
- Facial expressions
- Breathing patterns
- Spine and Shoulders

Just take a few minutes and use the AS IF principle if you haven't done this so far. Close your eyes and repeat "AS IF I know how to do that thing" or "AS IF I'M ____" and spend some time there to experience all the shifts in front of you. First, we'll have to start intentionally changing the four elements of AS IF. In a few days, you'll experience everything happening on autopilot and find yourself in the zone required for that moment. It all starts with changing our internal dialogue to 'AS IF I am ____", and the rest of the elements will follow. Use it regularly and see the new gates of opportunities and problem-solving open for you. Always remember -

> **"If plan A doesn't work, the alphabet has 25 more letters – 204 if you're in Japan"."**
>
> **CLAIRE COOK**

**Q.** What is the first scenario from your life you plan to use the "AS IF" in?

# Epilogue

First, an imaginary high-five from me to make it up to this point. Our minds have thousands of thoughts a day, and it's something that we do on autopilot. Just monitor when we find ourselves stuck in a cycle of overthinking, causing us to feel unpleasant, and keep our present (a gift) unwrapped. Are our own words (inner or spoken out loud) or the words of others causing us to create giant images in our heads? Regardless of what it is, we can bring our attention to the here and now using the learnings and exercises from the book and embrace being joyful and vibrant instead.

There is no such thing as not thinking, as "not having a thought right now" is a thought itself. It's all based on where we primarily focus in our lives, as that's what manifests in our realities.

> **"The mind is everything. What you think, you become."**
>
> **BUDDHA**

Ultimately, I'd like to bring our attention again to the "car mirrors' metaphor, adding the side-view mirror and sharing how all three relate to our life journey.

We learn from the side-view mirrors to focus and enjoy the present moment, appreciate what's around us on the left and the right, and look at the rearview mirror now and then to reflect on all the pleasant experiences from our past. Finally, we should keep our eyes on what's coming towards us in the future and ultimately embrace where we are headed in life. Focusing on three is crucial for successful driving, but the same is true for our lives.

We will all commit to working with the exercises in the book as and when required. Less than 1% of the 1440 minutes we all get in a day is all it needs to start making shifts in our lives.

Go through this book twice or thrice as every time you will notice something new you may have missed the first time as -

*Epilogue*

**"The book remains the same, but the reader changes and grows every time."**

Until next time, take good care of yourself, and keep smiling. Adios!

# About the Author

Japjot Kang is a smile generator and a hope creator. He's a business graduate who has become a mental wellness enthusiast. He's a Neuro-Linguistic Programming (NLP) master practitioner, a Mental Wellness Coach, and an Amazon's Best-Selling Author. He loves to help people struggling to manage their emotions make simple yet lasting changes in their lives. His mission in life is to reduce suffering, empower others, and make this planet a wonderful place to live in.

# *Books in this Series*

## Miraculous Phrases: 7 Untold Phrases to Instant Peace and Happiness

"Stop Wanting to be Happy or at Peace, Instead be Happy and at Peace NOW"

Everyone wants to be happy and at peace, but we are not told or taught in school how to go about or do it in a FAST manner. Use the short yet effective read with seven easy phrases and quick exercises to overcome negative thoughts, feelings and limiting beliefs and learn to instantly be happy and at peace.

*Books in this Series*

# Negative Thinking Banished: 7 Secrets to a Cheerful and Enthusiastic Self

"Get Unstuck, Be More, Do More and Embrace Positivity in your Life"

Everyone wants to bring more positivity into their lives, but how? Discover seven secrets and quick exercises to overcome past unpleasant memories and negative thoughts. Learn to unleash a cheerful and enthusiastic self in this short yet effective read.

# Mind-fullness to Mindfulness: 7 Fun Ways to Escape Chaos and Embrace Serenity

"Unlock your mind's potential: Break free from the mental chaos and embrace the serenity within."

Being mindful is crucial in today's fast-paced world. However, fully embracing mindfulness can be challenging when the world around us seems to encourage being mind-full instead. Take a moment to escape the chaos and embrace serenity now with this quick read.

# Books By The Author

## Self Confidence Unwrapped: 7 Exciting Ways to a Poised and Courageous Self

"Show up, stand out and seize your moment."

Which came first, the chicken or the egg, and does confidence in doing something come first or because of doing it over time? Demystify the latter with Self-Confidence Unwrapped and learn to Unleash a Poised and Courageous Self.

www.ingramcontent.com/pod-product-compliance
Lightning Source LLC
LaVergne TN
LVHW041556070526
838199LV00046B/1995